Truth
& Poetry
1 0 1

To Marge & Sherm
all the best
Aaron

Warren   Knox

Truth & Poetry 101

Covering (and uncovering)

Campus Goings-on in More

Than One Hundred Pieces

Of Light Verse

by

Warren Knox

with Drawings by the Author

A Minneola Press Book
P.O. Box 1796
Ojai, California 93024

Library of Congress Catalogue-in-Publication Data

Knox, Warren B.
Truth & Poetry 101

Library of Congress Catalogue Card Number

96-075346

ISBN 0-9640165-1-6

First Minneola Press paperback edition
April, 1996

1 3 5 7 9 10 8 6 4 2

For our sons, Charles and John

Warren   Knox

Several of the following
pieces were first published
in the **Wall Street Journal**,
the Ashland (Oregon) **Daily
Tidings**, and in promotional
materials for the **Central
Scientific Company**. Permis-
sion to reprint them is here
gratefully aknowledged.

4

Before We Begin

Miss Mary Maynard
Held forth in Sixth Grade
Where some of us studied
And most of us played

She gave us two truths
Which, alas, went unheeded:
A poem is a po-em;
And crisp rhyming is needed

Many years later
This one of us sees
Writing poems is a gift
Writing verse a disease

Miss Mary was right
Except for the rhyme-thing
Now po-ems are essays
And rhymes are a crime-thing

And so, gentle reader
The truth, if you please:
Just enjoy these verses
But don't catch the disease

Even Educated Hes and Shes Do It

Things around here
Should be calmer, by far
The dean just ran off
With the registrar

Their Days Might Be Numbered

Sad objects of
The world's derision
They never mastered
Long division

In dark and dingy
Dumps and dives
Dwelt those who couldn't
Do their "fives"

In debtor's prisons
Limehouse attics
Cringed those who failed
In mathematics

Today's math-flunkers
Fare better, to wit:
Hired by some college
They teach English Lit

Two Steps Sideways – March!

Three cheers for the College's
Planning Retreat
The tennis was great
There was plenty to eat

As for the planning
I can't quite remember
But I think we'll still open
This coming September

To a Private College

All hail thee, Eleemosynary
I'm glad you're not-for-profit, very
But to be absolutely veritable
I wish your alumni were a bit more charitable

* * * * * *

To a Public University

O   Monolith upon the hill
You're big and strong and wealthy, still
Precipitous the budget facts is
For them what lives or dies by taxes

Polish or Perish

Promotion, tenure - if you get it
Speak? Consult? Write books? Forget it!
The way to really make the scene
Is play golf, weekly, with the dean

What Do We Call Our Education Department?

Embry, Entom, Bi and Psych
Are prefix to a phrase we like
Every campus needs some Ge
Some Soci, Myth and Anthrop see?

We here offer no ap
For all of this ology
It just makes us sound better
Y'know. . . like... more collegey

Too Bad He Didn't Hear the Motion to Adjourn

He had a key to the Rare Book Room
And a Double-A parking sticker
A cabinet at the Faculty Club
Where he stored his cards and his liquor

He had his own locker in the gym
And his name on a library carrel
He had leather patches on both sleeves
Of his new tweedy jacket apparel

He seemed to have almost everything
But his perks all proved to be fleeting
He was only a first-year instructor who
Daydreamed during faculty meeting

Punt!

When his chairperson's turned autocratical
And the dean thinks his writing too radical
What's a poor guy to do
When his Fulbright falls through
And it's three years `til his next sabbatical?

Someone Said His Brother Was a Trustee

A more-than-you'd-think expenditure
With questionable resultant
Who fits the description? Well, who else?
The outside objective consultant

The study was "Teaching Effectiveness"
It's a goal all agreed was worth reaching
So consultant consulted with everyone
Except those who were doing the teaching

Never-Never Institute

It's MAIL ORDER COLLEGE
P.O. Box 26
To provide instant knowledge
And an ego quick-fix

It's fast food for thought
It's burgers and fries
It's a carnival con game
Where none get a prize

Just send all your money
Specify the degree
And soon, by return mail,
You're a new PhD

Get a drive-in diploma
To frame for your cravings
It costs self-respect
Not to mention life savings

No courses, no quizzes
And no dissertation
No labs and no lectures
- - - and no education

15

Plato Is O.K.

Thucydides and Dionysius
Your names are colorless and specious
Difficult to spell, pronounce
They don't have sparkle, zip or bounce

Your mothers were, alas, to blame
Who saddled you with tangled name
We'd do a better teaching job
If they had called you Al and Bob

Warren Knox

With a Special Pop-up Feature On the Faculty and Staff

In years past college catalogs
Held mainly course descriptions
Now they look more like magazines
What next? Ads and subscriptions?

Beware the Automatic Sprinklers

She often held her class outdoors
Where atmosphere was cooler
There were advantages, you see
To be a Summer Schooler

Sprawled on the lawn, beneath the trees
The Prof spoke more profoundly
And softly fanned by balmy breeze
Her students slept more soundly

Oratory in the Park

An on-leave sociologist
In London for a week
Wrote home to a colleague that
She fancied Hyde and Sikh

To Our Visiting Distinguished Professor
From the University of Leeds:

Get With the Programme

The rocky coast's splendour
The colour of sky
Down by the harbour
I ask myself why

As in labour and favour
All those added-on u's
That you English still savour
Can you give me some clues?

Do Brit authors (none better)
Ever think it absurd?
Oh — they're paid by the letter
And not by the wourd

SOC: Epidermis and Literature 1,2,3,4 and 5

Teaching ethnicity
Attracts electricity

The Lure Of Moonlighting If You're An Untenured Assistant Professor of Economics

One effect of an inflation
Not seen on any graph:
Now Econ pundit's four-bit words
Cost ten bucks and a half

Young Turks and Old Bones

There's this closeted skeleton
Said to be an old Prof
But at the suggestion
Most snicker or scoff

But then, there's this ring
They can't understand
Phi Beta Kappa,
Third phalange, right hand

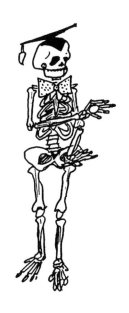

Two Senior Members of the Faculty
Discussing the Recent Election
Of a Former Student to The
Board of Trustees

"Rummy?"

"Quirky"

"Dummy?"

"Turkey"

"Income?"

"Scadly"

"Welcome?"

"Gladly!"

Why Sophomores Don't Eat In the Cafeteria

We want raspberry mousse
With lots of jousse
But we don't give a dingue
For jello meringue

A Victim of First-Year French

How does one turn a Moliere bolt?
(Instructions all in French)
Don't be a literary dolt
It's with a croissant wrench

The Campus Switchboard

My lips turned blue, my fingers cold
My face as white as death
`Cause when she asked if I'd please hold
I thought she meant my breath

I Don't Want a Party
Or
Please, Ms. Furneval, You've Been a Wonderful Assistant All These Years But I Don't Think I Can Take Even Just One More of Your Tuna Cheese Puffs

I have called in sick
And I've called in lame
I called when my kids
Had a big football game
And at sixty-five
If I haven't expired
I'll clean out my office
And call in retired

Warren Knox

A Recent Letter From the Retired Chairperson Of the Physical Education Department

I crossed the park the other day
Where, as a kid, I used to play
And lured by swings and rings and bars
I joined some Third Grade playground stars

On my old stunts I knew they'd suffer
(When I was young the kids were tougher)
Today, while they're all back in action
I'm lying here, in pain and traction

Thanks for the Memoiry

Tom Wolf and many others say,
"You can't go home on Alumni Day"
There are no more groves in Academe
All-Campus picnics are a faded dream
They've filled in the pond down by the mill
And planted dorms on Founder's Hill
Card catalog has turned to computer
Old-style librarians were quicker and cuter
Your mouths will have a bitter taste
You'll want to leave in sorry haste

But ignoring warnings, rather, we
Drank deep from the cup of memory
The old college spirit tasted the same
And so did the spirits after the game

A Fatal Virus

No lights, no hum, no clickety-click
I can hear my heart beat in the stillness
No words can be seen, anywhere on the screen
My PC has a terminal illness

31

When the President Returned
From a Power Seminar

"Too long I felt cowed
So I recently vowed
An intimidator to be

But so far it's not thrilling
Because now no one's willing
To be an intimidatee"

I Wouldn't Give You Two Scents

Real sheepskin diplomas
When new are quite smelly
Reminiscent of mutton
Without the mint jelly

Never a Bibliophile
Nor a Lender Be

The trouble with some books, by far
One seldom knows just where they are
They hide from one amongst the shelves
Or seem to vaporize themselves

Some colleague will drop by tomorrow
Request a certain book to borrow
"Yes, it's right here," one says, and then
Finds empty space where it had been

One constantly, then, deals in mystery
Of lost biography and history
Of absent Yeats and Keats and Twain
Of missing tomes on wine and Spain

Perhaps someday they'll come to light
Or sneak back home in dark of night
Meanwhile, one shrugs at reasons, rhymes
Now, pray, what happened to this morning's Times?

Warren   Knox

Why Parents of the Late Sixties Were Not In Favor of Coed Dorms

A lot of uses
Has the hanky
But best of all
It goes with panky

Why They Needn't Have Worried

Girls' cream and curlers
Boys' weekend stubbles
Soon burst all panky
Fear hubbubbles

Why He Missed the Departmental Dinner

His wife was nearly always at him
To windsor, ascot or cravat him
When, all of his defenses gone
He just went out and tied one on

Or Maybe It's the Hole In the Ozone Layer

Two simple reasons
Why freshmen can't read
They've been under-homeworked
And over-TV'd

Wisdom Comes Late

I read with horror of decisions
Made by Assistants in Admissions
Whose average age, or so I'm told
Is barely twenty-four years old

Some years ago, in like position
When I thumbs-upped or -downed admission
No fairer, wiser guy alive
But then of course, I was twenty-five

The Academic Procession

There's always one
Who's out of step
It's not tone-deafness
Or lack of pep

He marches thus
Lest we forget
To a different
Brass quartet

She Must Have Been a Hanoverian

A way to remember Stuart, Windsor and Tudor
Was attempted by Assistant Professor McGruder
But try as she might, couldn't rhyme Plantagenet
It's tough; I tried it; you can't imagine it.

This Will Probably Not Be On
The Final Examination

"So long, Pharaoh,"
Said the Great God Osiris
"Be seein' you
In the funnypapyrus"

Note to TAs and Readers:

Mark off 10 points if anyone
should refer to the Egyptian
Deity as "Oh, Cyrus!"

Why We Always Try to Arrive
A Little Late at the Stadium

Mr. Francis Scott Key
Pitched it too high for me
My voice is provoc'tive
For only an octave
My very worst scare
Is 'the rocket's red glare'
Though I keep on reaching
They're singing; I'm screeching

42

We Simply Must Address Curricular Reform

An obese reticulum
Is the curriculum
It's hard to treat
When it gets sickulum

Suggestions of purgery
Or open-heart surgery
Seem no more effective
Than witchcraft or scourgery

The final suggestion
Is really the best 'un
Form a committee
Then table the question

Listen Up, Budget Committee
Or
A Somewhat Over-Drawn Defense
Of the Research Budget
(Which Is Usually Overdrawn)

Whoever the genius that gave us the wheel
Tried thousands of times before it would squeal
The guy who came up with sandwich wrap
Didn't wait 'til the idea dropped in his lap
The paper clip person, the light bulb chap
Weren't hit by an instant-invention zap
It all took hard work, with no vacation
To produce what just <u>looked</u> like an inspiration

Power Failure

Two things that will power
Just cannot turn off:
Invocation hiccups;
Benediction cough

O Death, I Know a Sting When I See One

How still alive
Immortal Bard?
His players died
And most died hard

Like flies, they died
In staged malaise
Five nights a week
Plus matinees

And yet, Will lives
Long life unshaken
Cured ham, perhaps
Or was he Bacon?

Sabbatical Second Thoughts

Where lizard swims
And lava grows
And tortoise stands
Up on his toes

The reason only
Darwin knows
Why I picked the
Galapagos

No fresh water
No folks indigenous
Just flightless birds
And species originous

Of all my colleagues
Now alive
I'll be the fittest
(If I survive)

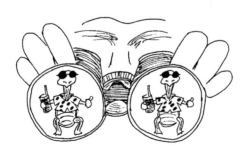

Taunt By the Classics Faculty On the Eve of Their Six-Person Football Challenge Game With the Athletic Department

You people may have new gymnasia
And modern recarpeted stadia
But we are all tenury
Sans doctoral penury
Moreover, we're just not afraid a' ya

Matching Funds Would Have Helped

Time and money beat the South
An oft-repeated headline
Lee didn't get the Grant — he missed
The application deadline

Chapter and Worse

A senior professor was promised
He could still teach one course, though retired
My Life With Authors, it's title
The subjects of which had expired

He thought of them all as his children
Hemingway, Faulkner and Buck
George Bernard Shaw was his "Gee Bee"
And Dickens, his favorite, "Chuck"

One day from his personal copy
Of New Testament, one TA claims
He read to the class some selections
Using only familiar names

It was all a big joke to his students
Until the discovery that
Right there on the fly-leaf was written
Best wishes, Old Buddy, from Matt

Calling Dr. Newton

A professor of Physics named Brown
Taught that all that goes up must come down
But his theory exploded; the rocket was loaded
He's in orbit 10 miles above town

Professional Prerogative
With a Purpose

I've lately decided
To give A's and B's
'Cause my C and D students
Come back as Trustees

Choose Any Three For a Nickel

Our house is overrun with books
They're crammed in crannies, jammed in nooks
They're overflowing shelves and racks
Stacked up in closets, stuffed in cracks
They're piled on chairs and under tables
Stored in basement, attic, gables
Sprawling, crawling, nesting, roosting
It sometimes seems they're reproducing
The process simply must reverse
Restore the order; stop the curse

Ha! We'll clear space for desk and `phone
Then start a Book Club of our own

The Dean's First Mistake

She'd invited a few
Of the faculty in
For a sherry
At their new apartment

"Are we having mixed nuts?"
He, hopefully, asked
She said, "No, just the
English Department"

A Thinking Man's Multiversity

We have a School of Medicine
Of Nursing and of Business
The latter quite respected for
Producing Kids of Whizness

A School of Forestry, of Law
Biology, Marine
(That boasts a school of porpoises,
With equal seldom seen)

We have a School of Dentistry,
Architecture being sought
But I wish we could find donors for
Some current Schools of Thought

I'm Thinking of Changing My Major

Athenian logic
Makes my brain hodge-pogic
And so does reliance
On Socratic Science

Before graduation
Who'll be my salvation?
If not Aristotle
Maybe Sir Walter Scott'll

The New Associate Provost

His purple prose
Seemed only fittin'
With a middle name
Like Bulwer-Lytton

Why Doesn't He Just Dance With His Own Wife?

At the President's Ball
All the wives take a chance
The ladies, afraid,
That he'll ask them to dance

He always proceeds
To step on their shoes
It's so hard to waltz
To Rhythm and Blues

Plus a Car and Throat Spray Money

If you think football coaches would kill for a fullback
And chase kids from Vermont to Montana
You've never seen a hungry choral director
Stalk a prize baritone or soprana

59

The Year Oscar Went Wilde

We had a most traditional
Department of the Drama
Some years they gave "Pygmalion"
Some "I Remember Mama"

So when we asked they take a chance
And stage more modern journey
They mustered all their courage for
"The Importance of Being Ernie"

It Doesn't Take One to Know One

Most campus "intellectuals"
Seem stubborn, rude and skeptical
Caused, one might suspect, by being
Unloved and dyspeptical

A Brief Chronology
Of Tenured Professorial Dress

1955 Comfortable jacket
      Well padded and tweeded
      Suede patches at elbows
      (Wanted, not needed)

1965 Lumpy and bumpy
      In sandals and sweatshirt
      And during the summer
      A see-through fishnet shirt

1975 Electric blue stretch pants
      Sweater made for a turtle
      And if that doesn't get it
      Then a blue-collar shirt' ll

1985 Soft balloon trousers
      Wide stripes and red braces
      Ne're changing their stripe
      Nor getting red faces

1995 No longer constrained
      By the need to be cute
      It's a new fashion bombshell:
      A nice gray business suit

Warren Knox

And a New Headache For Librarians

His name was "Pre-1925 German Naval Encodinq Systems,"
Hers, "A Collection of 19th Century French Poets"
They were shelved side by side
And neither could hide
A strong mutual attraction, though they couldn't show it

He boasted 672 pages plus a glossary,
She, a mere 124 with notations in both French and English
Propriety provided
And they quickly decided
It was immoral to be living together and remain singlish

It might have been more than a marriage of convenience
And, except for traditional academic fears and anguishes
A true affair of the heart
It could have been the start
Of a beautiful Combined Department of Germanic &
Romance Languages

Author's note:

Never mind the meter
on this one; just
work on the concept

The Education of Faculty Children: A Trade Imbalance

Tuition exchange
Isn't working, that's clear
Ours want to go there
But theirs won't come here

64

W a r r e n   K n o x

No Substitutes Accepted

A parrot was perched in Zoology Lab
The most regal that one ever saw
You could tell, well enough,
That he wasn't just stuffed
Rather, he was the real McCaw

The Campus Bookstore

Back behind the T-shirts
And the posters and the steins
Behind the shades and razor blades
Mouthwash and valentines
Beyond the fluffy animals
Where students rarely tread
In searching for potato chips
I found a book instead

It Can't Be the Food

A neat place, the campus infirmary
Its occupants mainly short-termary
They check into bed
Just'ere mid-terms, it's said
With illnesses most non-confirmary

Perhaps Just a Certificate

With honorary-type degrees
We've never learned to "hood" with ease
This seeming harmless piece of cloth
Turns into Goth or Visigoth

In hands of president and dean
It's now alive and serpentine
It catches under chin or nose
Or flips bifocals many rows

In spite of help from platform folks
It near decapitates or chokes
Often it's occurred to me
That nowadays we backwards be

Some excercises old and far
(In some ways very similar)
In setting serious and wooded
The **executioners** were hooded

Stuck For An Answer

Faculty "brown bag" lunch discussions
Quite often are failures, utter
It may be because some arrogant cuss
Holds down the floor `gainst the rest of us
Or maybe because it's hard to dis-cuss
With a mouth full of peanut butter

Warren   Knox

How Do You Name a Building?

It sounds like such an easy task
Depends, of course, on who you ask
Request suggestions, wait for the mail
What could be simpler? How could it fail?

Our millionaire, one Angus McPhee,
Had been a leading nominee
Until his heirs (without our knowledge)
Made a deal with another college

Then there was Dean Lysander Yost
He flunked the least, and pleased the most
At eighty-three was still a power
And then he died during Happy Hour

President Toote, no longer alive
Was our Founder, back in `95
Support for him had taken root
And in the vanguard, Mrs. Toote

Alumni view was split; when polled
Some wanted old Professor Gold
Others touted Coach Pudge Hicks
Whose team trounced Yale in `26

The choices stacked up, score on score
By letter, telegram, what's more
Torchlight rallies and incantations
Sit-ins, strikes and demonstrations

Thus battle raged, back'rd and for'd
We knew the decision was up to the Board
They stepped right in and, of all the gall,
They named our new building "Trustees Hall"

Liberte! Egalite! Off-campus Apartment!
Or
Beware of Greeks Bearing Kegs

They're closing down some of the dorms, 'tis said
But one spot is as good as another
When a dozen RAs can't take the place
Of one good old-fashioned House Mother

Pretend You're In a Hurry, Here Comes a Philosopher

Among life's great questions
Which cause the most stress
Are those we must answer
With "no"or with "yes"

His Signature Resembled an Ink Blot

Can poor innocent freshman be faulted
If his search for himself is soon halted?
When he starts off in Psych
He can't know what it's like
To be Freuded and Junged and Gestalted

Warren   Knox

Overheard During the Morning Coffee Break At The National Conference for College and University Buildings & Grounds Superintendents

"I tried that new grass from the Argentine pampas"
Said the man from a small, private midwestern campas

But the one from South State, predictably pompous,
Said, "Y'all couldn't **qive** me such lawn for my compous"

The Multi-branch U guy, to quell any rumpuses
Said, "We use different turf for **each** of our cumpuses" *

*LAT: cumpi

No Stomach For It

A zoology student named Bart
While trying to locate the heart
Cut the dorsal aorta
Which proved to him, sorta
He should be in Psych or in Art

He Took It With Him

More than tenure
And more than fame
His Nobel Prize
Or household name

Throughout his life
And unto Grace
He valued most
His parking space

He Should Have Asked
for an Incomplete

Here lies the body
Of big Jim Slade
The man who invented
The Pass-Fail grade

He went to his grave
Of honor bereft
Renounced by his colleagues
Who gave him an F

Warren   Knox

Overheard In the Faculty Lounge

In this age of computers
I'm telling you, neighbor
My word processor still is
An Eberhard-Faber

He Was Her TA in Graduate School

Two eminent historians
In private life were married
And through the years their own careers
Back home at night ne're carried

They published, oft, opposing views
Stooped not to Ladies Firstery
But she monogrammed the bathroom towels
With HIStory and HERStory

Registration By the Numbers

"Don't worry," said the registrar
Computers' brains are best by far
Those long, long lines will disappear
That start down there and end up here

"We'll send their schedules out by mail
The system simply cannot fail"
But lines are back and not so strange is
Computers can't handle requests for changes

Love In the Cafeteria Kitchen

The way to man's heart's through his stomach
Lorraine was quite sure of it when
He ate her cheese pies, then looked in her eyes
And whispered, "Please quiche me again"

Do I Get Any Credit For Remedial Chem?

A flameout in his Bunsen burner
He reached for soda, careless learner
And grabbed instead the Carbon Tet
His eyebrows aren't grown in as yet

An Example of Infinite Wisdom

In temporary
Residence
Are chancellors
And presidents

Dinner At The Chairperson's

Hostess's directions
Told, clearly, the route
But house number was missing
And porch light burned out
We asked door to door
`Til at last got it right
Then found that the dinner
Was <u>next</u> Saturday night

What Should We Wear to the Reception
For the Spanish Ambassador Next Week?

We'd gussied up in days gone by
In formal dress - stiff shirt, black tie
To take the Concert Season in

Tonight, still formal-garbed, long-gowned
We ponder as we look around
Have we committed social sin?

An usher, jeans-attired, looks down
Spies us, and smile turns into frown
Good grief, he thinks, who let <u>them</u> in?

Warren   Knox

News Item:

The Alumni Society will hold this year's Executive
Committee dinner in the Rare Book Room of Memorial
Library.

A banquet in the Rare Book Room
Suggests exotic fare
All bound in hide, one must decide
Not how to start, but where

The appetizers, page by page
Could come from **War and Peace**
And then, for soup, a spicy group
Of **Odes of Ancient Greece**

The entrees? Here, in **Reader's Guide**
They give great choice, you see
One's taste can play from A through K
Or else from L through Z

Now comes dessert if you're `a mind
Walt Whitman, leaf by leaf
Or if distressed try Edgar Guest
(He's light beyond belief)

For those who like a little snack
Ten minutes after dinner
Try **Papal Sees**; they're good with cheese
Besides, the paper's thinner

Last, **Sonnets from the Portuqese**
Or **Ballads from the Welsh**
Produce a very literary
After-dinner belch

The Final Gun

Ascended taut
Descended limp
Timekeeper shot
The Goodyear blimp

Rx For Happier Times
And a Healthier Scalp

Truth or poetry; poetry or truth
You needn't choose which that you `druther
Both have elements common to each
And a little of one in the other

Maybe it takes the two, together
(Always shake well before swallowing)
The mixture might help some human ills
Like, for example, the following:

Hives and warts and dermatitis
And bites of various bug-types
Chills and bunions and tonsilitis
And small crawly-under-the-rug-types

Headaches and hang-nails, hay fever and gout
Guaranteed not to get any worse
If you but try, your best not to lie
And express yourself, lightly, in verse

Remember To Smile

I suggest a Faculty Telephone Book
With a photo in every space
For we who have trouble remembering names
But who never forget a face

Pray For the Preident's Stomach

Impending surgery was due
All strength and courage then
He mustered

To face, alone and unafraid,
Two weeks of jello, cottage cheese
And custard

Advice For The New Coach

A grain of salt will always help
No matter what they feed ya
The "they" to whom I here refer:
Alumni and the meedya

You Remember Good Old
Professor What's-His-Name

You Don't?

Emeritus, at last, am I
But not without some perks
An office in the basement with
Steam heat that sometimes works

They let me post my office hours
A gesture that is kindly
But I'm behind the boiler and
Someone has yet to find me

A reference in the catalog
With others of my sort
A pre-obituary list
In type-size thin and short

I'm welcome over at The Club
But things just aren't the same
The hostess is the only one
Who calls me by my name

One bright side of emeritry —
The nice development folks
Who call me with regularity
And tell me annuity jokes

I should go and see the president
(Though I'm beyond beseeching)
I'd tell him, "Thank you very much,
But I'd sooner still be teaching"

In Case of Higher Degrees

How did he manage to keep cool
Through muggy heat and endless speakers?
Underneath his academic gown
Were T-shirt, bathing trunks and sneakers

Warren   Knox

In The Next World

I long for a life without publishing strife
Without intra-departmental schemes
No tenure allowed for the Young Turk crowd
No presidents, trustees or deans

A nice quiet place where one needn't face
Either Art Club or Founder's Day greetings
A place of committees without any chairs
And of five-minute faculty meetings

No National Merits or Magna cum Parrots
No alumni or grade-changing static
There'll just be a candle, big print I can handle
And some space in the Library attic

This book was typeset using QuarkXpress in
a macintosh computer. Typefaces are: Journal, Franklin Gothic, and
Monotype Typewriter Gothic.

Cover Photography & Book design:
F. Schnaas